Rookie
Read-About® Science

✓ P9-DND-946

What Is Matter?

By Don L. Curry

Consultant
Linda Bullock
Science Curriculum Specialist

Children's Press®
A Division of Scholastic Inc.
New York   Toronto   London   Auckland   Sydney
Mexico City   New Delhi   Hong Kong
Danbury, Connecticut

Designer: Herman Adler Design
Photo Researcher: Caroline Anderson
The photo on the cover shows a boy drinking from a sports bottle.

Library of Congress Cataloging-in-Publication Data

Curry, Don L.
  What is matter? / by Don L. Curry ; consultant, Linda Bullock.
    p. cm. — (Rookie read-about science)
  Includes index.
  ISBN 0-516-23620-2 (lib. bdg.)   0-516-24667-4 (pbk.)
  1. Matter—Juvenile literature. I. Title. II. Series.
  QC173.36.C87 2004
  530—dc22

                       2004001223

CHILDREN'S PRESS, and ROOKIE READ-ABOUT®,
and associated logos are trademarks and or registered trademarks
of Scholastic Library Publishing. SCHOLASTIC and associated logos
are trademarks and or registered trademarks of Scholastic Inc.
12 13 14 R 13

What is matter?

Matter is solid, liquid, or gas.

Matter is everywhere you go. It can look like this.

Matter can look like this,

or this,

or this.

Matter can look like
this, too.

Matter can also look
like this.

A bat and baseball are made of matter. The air inside a balloon is made of matter.

The water from a drinking
fountain is made of matter.

Some matter is solid.

Can you name the kinds of matter you see here?

Solid matter has its own shape. The shape of solid matter is hard to change.

You can change the shape
of solid matter. But it is
hard to change it back to
what it was.

Some matter is liquid, too.

Can you name the other
kinds of matter you
see here?

Liquid matter does not have a shape of its own. Liquid matter can be any shape.

Its shape changes each time it is put inside something new.

Some matter is gas. You can't always see a gas.

Look closely!

How do you know the gas is there?

Matter that is gas does not have a shape of its own. It can be any shape.

A gas spreads out in whatever space it is in.

Sometimes matter is hard, like a baseball bat.

solid

Sometimes matter is wet
and pours from a bottle.
Sometimes matter fills
a balloon.

liquid

gas

Everything is made of matter. That means everything you can see, feel, taste, and touch.

It even means you. You are made of matter, too.

Words You Know

gas

liquid

matter

shape

solid

31

Index

About the Author

Don L. Curry is a writer, editor, and educational consultant who lives and works in New York City. Don taught for 10 years and has now written more than 50 books on various science topics. When he is not writing, he can often be found in Central Park reading or looking at the science exhibits at the Museum of Natural History.

Photo Credits

Photographs © 2004: Corbis Images/Bob Rowan/Progressive Image: 22; Getty Images: 16 (Stephen Chernin), 21, 27 left, 30 top right (Antonio Luiz Hamdan); James Levin/Studio 10: cover, 3, 4, 5, 6, 7 top, 7 bottom, 9, 12, 14, 15, 17, 18, 25, 26, 27 right, 29, 30 top left, 30 bottom, 31 bottom, 31 top; PhotoEdit/ Richard Hutchings: 11; PictureQuest/SW Productions/Photodisc: 13.